Rookie
Read-About®
Science

The Moon

by Cody Crane

Content Consultant

Kevin Manning

Astronomer

Reading Consultant

Jeanne M. Clidas, Ph.D.

Reading Specialist

Children's Press®

An Imprint of Scholastic Inc.

Library of Congress Cataloging-in-Publication Data
A CIP catalog record of this book is available from the
Library of Congress

Produced by Spooky Cheetah Press
Art Direction: Tom Carling, Carling Design Inc.
Creative Direction: Judith Christ-Lafond for Scholastic

Published in 2018 by Children's Press, an imprint of
Scholastic Inc.

Printed in Heshan, China 62

SCHOLASTIC, CHILDREN'S PRESS, ROOKIE
READ-ABOUT SCIENCE™, and associated logos
are trademarks and/or registered trademarks of
Scholastic Inc..

1 2 3 4 5 6 7 8 9 10 R 27 26 25 24 23 22 21 20 19 18

Photographs ©:cover: Somchai Som/Shutterstock;
back cover: jakkapan21/iStockphoto; cartoon dog
throughout: Kelly Kennedy; 1: JSC/NASA; 2-3:
Klagyivik Viktor/Shutterstock; 4-5: DWPhoto/Getty
Images; 6: Richard Wahlstrom/Getty Images; 8-9
background: ThierryHennet/Getty Images; 9 inset:
Photodynamic/Getty Images; 10: Goddard Space
Flight Center/Arizona State University/NASA; 11
background: Clearviewstock/Dreamstime; 11 moon:
Buyenlarge/Getty Images; 12-13: Magictorch; 14:
jakkapan21/iStockphoto; 15: ttsz/Getty Images; 16:
Torsak/Dreamstime; 17 illustrations: Gary Hincks/
Science Source; 17 background: Clearviewstock/
Dreamstime; 18: AZP Worldwide/Shutterstock; 20:
John Kaufmann/NASA; 21: SuperStock/age fotostock;
22-23: artpartner-images/Getty Images; 24: NASA;
25: Michael Dunning/Getty Images; 26 center:
Daniel Valla FRPS/Alamy Images; 26 background:
Clearviewstock/Dreamstime; 27 : JSC/NASA; 28-29, 31
center top: Aimee Herring; 28-29 paper clips: Angela
Jones/Dreamstime; 28-29 graph paper: Natbasil/
Dreamstime; 30 background: Giraphics/Dreamstime;
30 right: mylisa/Shutterstock; 30 left: Ivy Close
Images/Alamy Images; 31 bottom: artpartner-images/
Getty Images; 31 top: JSC/NASA; 31 center bottom:
Magictorch; 32: Richard Wahlstrom/Getty Images.

Scholastic Inc., 557 Broadway, New York, NY 10012.

Table of Contents

Let's Explore the Moon!

The moon is Earth's nearest neighbor. It is a large ball of rock. It **orbits** our planet. You can often see the moon shining in the night sky. Sometimes you can even spot the moon during the day.

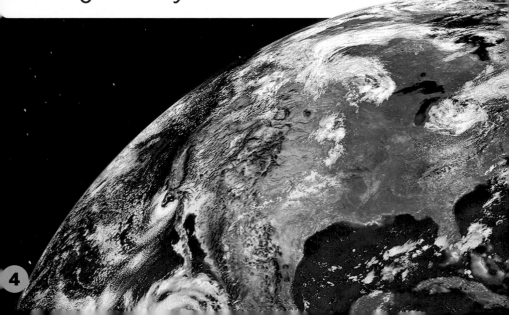

From the moon, Earth looks like a giant blue-and-white marble.

Our Moon

The moon is gray and dusty.
Nothing lives there. There is no
flowing water. The moon has
almost no **atmosphere**. So there
is no air to breathe. There is no
wind to blow or any weather at all.
Nothing on the moon ever washes
or blows away. So its surface
almost never changes.

The hottest temperature ever recorded on Earth was 134°F (56.7°C). It was recorded in Death Valley National Park, California.

The moon can be twice as warm as the hottest desert on Earth.

Death Valley

An atmosphere keeps a place from getting too hot or too cold. The moon does not have that protection. The sun's rays heat the moon during the day. Temperatures can be hotter than that of boiling water. At night, the moon is freezing cold. Temperatures can be twice as cold as in icy Antarctica, the coldest place on Earth.

Antarctica

The coldest temperature recorded on Earth was -135°F (-94°C). It was recorded in Antarctica.

Rocks whizzing through space hit the moon. They left behind millions of craters. The crashes also caused rock to be thrown from the craters. Those formed the moon's mountains.

Long ago, there were also volcanoes on the moon. Hot melted rock called lava flowed out of them. The lava cooled into smooth plains called "seas."

This mountain is in the Tycho crater. It is more than a mile high. That is one-fifth as tall as Mount Everest.

2

A Place in Space

The sun is the center of our solar system. Eight planets travel around the sun. A moon is an object that orbits a planet. Our moon travels around Earth. There are many other moons in our solar system.

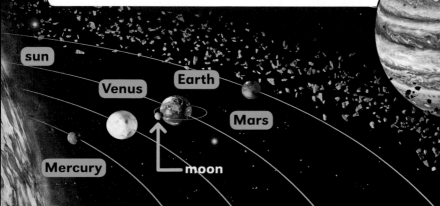

sun

Venus

Earth

Mars

Mercury

moon

Jupiter

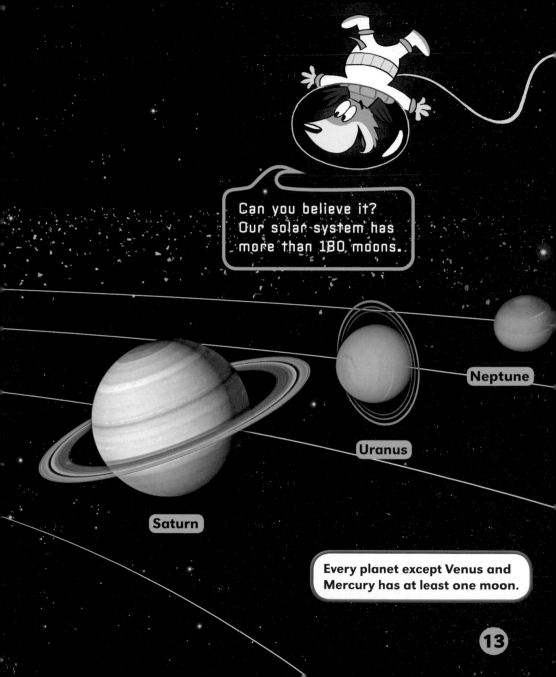

Can you believe it?
Our solar system has
more than 180 moons.

Neptune

Uranus

Saturn

Every planet except Venus and
Mercury has at least one moon.

13

Earth's **gravity** pulls on the moon. That is what keeps the moon close by and orbiting our planet. The moon has gravity, too. It is much smaller than Earth, though. It does not have enough gravity to move the entire planet! The moon does have just enough gravity to tug on Earth's oceans. That causes their waters to rise and fall. This is called the tide.

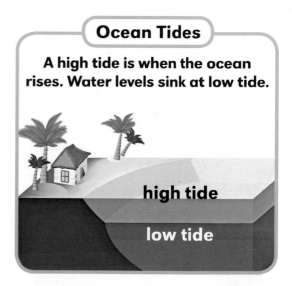

Ocean Tides

A high tide is when the ocean rises. Water levels sink at low tide.

high tide

low tide

Some scientists think the moon came from Earth. A large space rock may have hit Earth when the planet was forming. Chunks of rock flew into space. Some pieces gathered into a ball. They became the moon.

Imagine if Earth were the size of a basketball. The moon would be the size of a tennis ball.

The Moon Is Born

This diagram shows how scientists think the moon was formed.

1 A very large object crashed into Earth.

2 Materials from the object and Earth's surface flew out into space.

3 The materials began orbiting Earth and formed a disk.

4 Eventually, the materials became a round shape.

5 The newly formed moon began orbiting Earth.

6 Today, the moon is Earth's closest companion.

The surface of the moon acts like a mirror. Light from the sun bounces off the moon, making it look bright.

The View from Earth

The moon looks big. That is because it is so near Earth. Stars are bigger than the moon. They look small because they are farther away.

Some people see patterns on the moon— like a face or a rabbit.

The moon also looks bright. It does not make its own light, though.

The Aitken basin is the largest crater on the moon.

The moon takes about 27 days to orbit Earth. The moon spins like a top as it circles the planet. Each spin also takes about 27 days. That timing causes the same side of the moon to always face Earth. The side we see is called the near side. We cannot see the back half of the moon. It is called the far side.

The moon and Earth are both really old. They formed 4.5 billion years ago!

This photo shows the far side of the moon with Earth in the distance.

waxing crescent · first quarter · waxing gibbous · full moon

The moon seems to change shape during the month as it travels around Earth. But it is not really changing shape. As the moon moves, the lit portion we can see changes.

waning gibbous

last quarter

waning crescent

new moon

That creates the moon's **phases**. During a full moon, we can see one whole side lit up. Light hits the back side of the moon during a new moon. Then we cannot see the moon at all.

Going to the Moon

In 1969, Neil Armstrong became the first person to walk on the moon. He, Buzz Aldrin, and Michael Collins were part of the *Apollo 11* mission. When Armstrong stepped on the moon, he said, "That's one small step for man, one giant leap for mankind."

On July 16, 1969, *Apollo 11* blasted into space.

24

Armstrong and Aldrin planted an American flag on the moon.

Footprints left on the moon in 1969 are still there.

Astronaut Equipment

This is the space suit used by the *Apollo 11* astronauts.

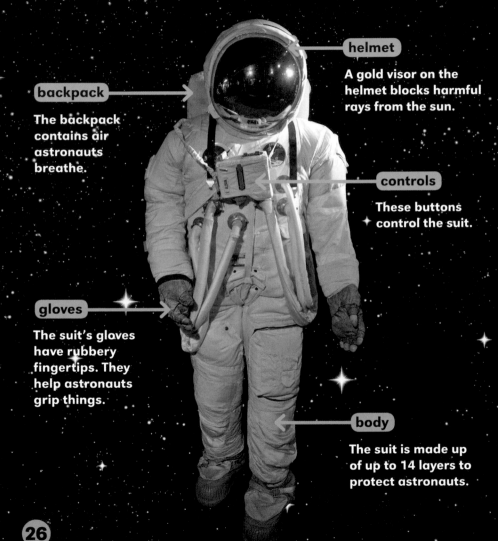

helmet

A gold visor on the helmet blocks harmful rays from the sun.

backpack

The backpack contains air astronauts breathe.

controls

These buttons control the suit.

gloves

The suit's gloves have rubbery fingertips. They help astronauts grip things.

body

The suit is made up of up to 14 layers to protect astronauts.

26

A special Lunar Roving Vehicle allowed astronauts to drive on the moon.

It took the *Apollo 11* team three days to reach the moon in a rocket. The team spent about 21 hours on the moon before heading back to Earth.

Ten other people have visited the moon since then. The last trip was made in 1972.

More astronauts could go to the moon someday. Maybe one of them will be you!

Make Moon Craters

Find out what causes some craters to be bigger than others. Be sure to ask an adult for help!

YOU WILL NEED:
- ✓ Large baking pan
- ✓ Flour
- ✓ Marble
- ✓ Tape measure
- ✓ Ruler
- ✓ Pencil and paper
- ✓ Ping-Pong ball
- ✓ Golf ball

STEP-BY-STEP:

1 Pour flour into the pan to form a layer about 2 inches (5 centimeters) deep. Shake the pan to smooth out the flour.

2 Hold the marble 1 foot (30 centimeters) above the flour. Drop the marble into the flour.

3

Carefully pick up the marble. Measure the size of the crater left behind. Measure how wide and deep it is. Record your results.

4

Shake the pan to make the flour smooth again.

5 Continue dropping different balls from different heights into the pan. Measure the craters and record your results.

Think About It:
How does the size of an object, as well as the height from which it is dropped, affect the crater it makes?

Stories About the Moon

People have always wondered about the moon. They made up stories about it. Here are two examples:

★ People joke that the moon is made of cheese. That is because its craters make the moon look like Swiss cheese!

★ Khonsu (**kon**-su) is the ancient Egyptian god of the moon. His name means "traveler." That's because the moon travels across the sky each night.

Khonsu is often shown with the moon over his head.

Glossary

atmosphere (**at**-muhs-feer): layer of gases that surrounds a planet

gravity (**grav**-i-tee): force that pulls things toward the center of Earth and keeps them from floating away

orbits (**or**-bits): travels in a circular path around a planet or the sun

phases (**fazes**): stages of the moon's change in shape as it appears from Earth

Index

Facts for Now

Visit this Scholastic Web site for more information
on the moon:
www.factsfornow.scholastic.com
Enter the keyword Moon

About the Author

Cody Crane is an award-winning nonfiction children's writer.
From a young age, she was set on becoming a scientist. She later
discovered that writing about science could be just as fun as the
real thing. She lives in Houston, Texas, with her husband and son.